IMAGES OF WAR

AMERICAN EXPEDITIONARY FORCE

FRANCE 1917-1918

RARE PHOTOGRAPHS FROM WARTIME ARCHIVES

JACK HOLROYD

Pen & Sword
MILITARY

First published in Great Britain in 2012 by
PEN & SWORD MILITARY
an imprint of
Pen & Sword Books Ltd,
47 Church Street, Barnsley,
South Yorkshire.
S70 2AS

Copyright © Jack Holroyd, 2012

ISBN 9781 84884 877 1

Printed and bound in Great Britain by CPI UK

Pen & Sword Books Ltd incorporates the imprints of
Pen & Sword Aviation, Pen & Sword Maritime,
Pen & Sword Military, Pen & Sword Select, Pen & Sword Military Classics,
Leo Cooper, Wharncliffe Local History

For a complete list of Pen & Sword titles please contact:
PEN & SWORD BOOKS LIMITED
47 Church Street, Barnsley, South Yorkshire, S70 2AS, England.
E-mail: enquiries@pen-and-sword.co.uk
Website: www.pen-and-sword.co.uk

Contents

Introduction

CONFLICT ERUPTED IN EUROPE in August 1914 and the President of the United States, Woodrow Wilson, promptly declared America's neutrality. Despite strong ties with Britain, Wilson was concerned about American citizens who had been born in Germany and Austria. Consequently he proposed an even-handed approach towards all the belligerent stating that it was to be maintained in both 'thought and deed'. The President steadfastly held to his hope of a peaceful solution to the conflict despite the protestations of those convinced that events in Europe would inevitably draw America into the war. He was supported in his policy of non-involvement by some politicians who argued strongly in favour of the USA maintaining its isolationist policy. This included the pacifist pressure group, the American Union Against Militarism. In 1916, Wilson campaigned for re-election on a peace platform with the slogan 'He kept us out of war'.

Opinion against Germany hardened after the sinking of the *Lusitania*. William J. Bryan, the pacifist Secretary of State, resigned and Wilson replaced him with the pro-Allied Robert Lansing. At that time Wilson announced an increase in the size of the US armed forces. Of the 139 US citizens aboard *Lusitania*, 128 lost their lives, and there was massive outrage in Britain and America. The British felt that the Americans just had to declare war on Germany. However, US President Woodrow Wilson refused to overreact. He said at Philadelphia on 10 May 1915: 'There is such a thing as a man being too proud to fight. There is such a thing as a nation being so right that it does not need to convince others by force that it is right.' It would be two years before the United States declared war on the German government (not the German people).

A drastic ploy was concocted by the Germans to ensure that America did not enter the war on the side of the Allies. They surmised that should the United States become embroiled in a fight on their own doorstep then likelihood of their intervention in the fighting in France would diminish. German Foreign Minister, Alfred Zimmerman, attempted to provoke Mexico and Japan into attacking the United States with the promise of German assistance after the fight with Russia was successfully ended. A message containing Zimmerman's intent was decoded by the British and immediately sent to the US, further swaying the Americans to action.

Due primarily to unrestricted submarine warfare conducted by Germany and the Zimmerman note, President Wilson asked Congress for permission to go to war, and on 6 April, 1917, congress officially declared it. President Wilson, along with many Americans, justified their involvement as: 'an act of high principle and idealism...[and]...as a crusade to make the world safe for democracy'.

With that declaration, and preliminary steps under way to put the nation on a war footing; delegations began to arrive. The first of these were the British and the

French. Italian, Belgian and Japanese missions followed. The Senate and House passed the army draft bill which allowed for the calling up of ten million men between the ages of twenty-one and thirty-one. The French and the British were asking for the immediate despatch of American troops to France. To comply with the clamour for help, the War Department announced that nine regiments of engineers would be raised immediately and shipped out. The President ordered the 1st Division of the regular standing army to France under command of Major-General Pershing.

The 1st Division, American Expeditionary Force (AEF), landed in France in June 1917. The 2nd Division did not arrive until September and by 31 October 1917, the AEF only numbered 6,064 officers and 80,969 men. Nine months after war was declared there were 175,000 American troops in Europe. This was nowhere near the half a million plus that Britain had put into the fight in the same length of time in 1914. Consequently, despite her strength on paper, America was in no position to influence the Allied war activities in 1917.

However, was America to blame for the lack of speed in her military build-up? Whereas Britain had spent time in 1914 planning for war and creating six divisions for the European campaign, America was all but starting from scratch. In peacetime, the American army only numbered 190,000 and they were spread across America. Now, with the declaration of war, these men had to move to the eastern seaboard where many camps had to be built to accommodate them before they sailed across the Atlantic. French ports had to be greatly expanded to handle the influx of men and the French rail network in the region had to be improved.

Pershing wanted the AEF to be ready for combat. He certainly did not want what the British and French were expecting; that the AEF be used to fill in where the Allies were weak. The American commander-in-chief wanted an independent fighting army that was self-contained. Therefore, when the Germans launched their great offensive of March 1918, there was only one American division in the Allied lines – with three divisions in training areas. The series of German offensives beginning in March 1918 posed serious dangers to the French and British. Paris was threatened and on two occasions, the British were nearly driven back to the Channel, but in these defensive battles the AEF played little part.

However, the German spring offensive had made Pershing realise that he needed to change his course of action. In June it was agreed that American troops would be sent to France from America without space-occupying equipment that could be provided by the French and British once the Americans were in France. In June and July 1918, America sent over 584,000 men. The German army could not hope to cope with such numbers now taking the field against them.

In July 1918, the French launched a major attack against the Germans from the Forest of Villers-Cotterêts, this attack included two American divisions – a total of 54,000 men. By August 1918, there were upwards of one and a half million

American troops in France. In that month the British and French began their One Hundred Days' Offensive, or 'Advance to Victory'. This led to the smashing of the Hindenburg Line, capture of ground beyond, and the Armistice in November 1918.

Taylor collection

The excellent picture book *U.S. Official Pictures of the World War* was published in 1920 by Pictorial Bureau, written and compiled by James C. Russell and William E. Moore and was with the co-operation and collaboration of fifteen contributors. Around 900 images taken by the photographers of the Signal Corps tell the story of the American Expeditionary Force in France and a selection has been made from these. Additional illustrations have been included from the Taylor Library to help the pictorial history, and they, along with images from the ninety-year-old book, will reintroduce to public awareness the crafted camera work of those days of the Great War. This *Images of War* publication will serve as a catalogue for illustrations now available in the Taylor archive. An identifying number is included with the captions.

The kind of image that helped the United States enter the war. Unrestricted submarine warfare and the loss of American lives caused a shift in opinion in the States. The original caption reads: *These pictures just received in this country tell part of the story of the sinking of the French liner Sontay in the Mediterranean on 10 April with a loss of forty-five lives.* **THE NEW YORK TIMES MID-WEEK PICTORIAL WWI/US001**

Chapter One

'We Go To War'—April 1917

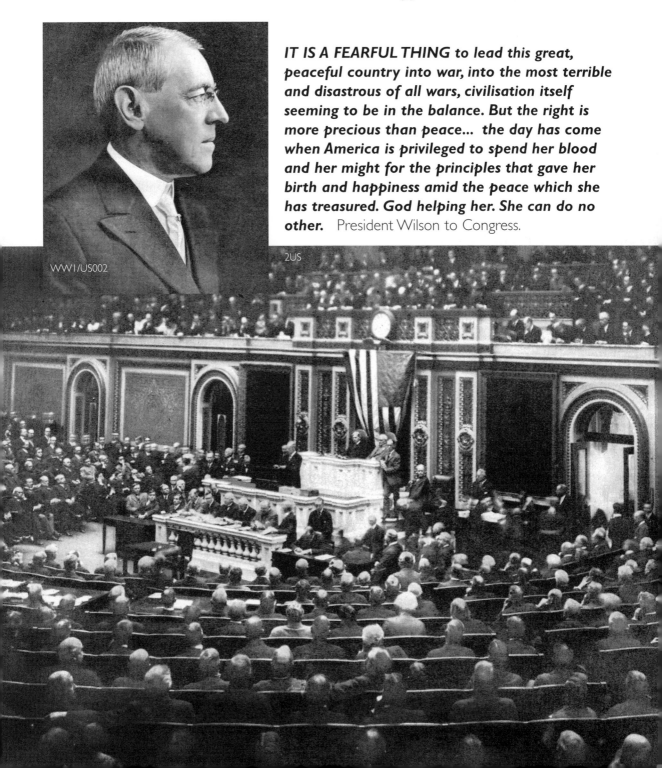

IT IS A FEARFUL THING to lead this great, peaceful country into war, into the most terrible and disastrous of all wars, civilisation itself seeming to be in the balance. But the right is more precious than peace... the day has come when America is privileged to spend her blood and her might for the principles that gave her birth and happiness amid the peace which she has treasured. God helping her. She can do no other. President Wilson to Congress.

WWI/US002

2US

At 8.30 pm, 2 April 1917, President Wilson appeared before Congress, sitting in joint session, and read his message recommending that a state of war be declared to exist between the United States and the Imperial German Government. The war resolution was passed by the Senate 4 April and by the House 6 April 1917. It was signed by the President and became effective the same day.

Top: Outside the National Guard Armoury in New York City when the call went out for the first volunteers. 4US
Above: Seventh Regiment, Illinois National Guard, Chicago leaving for camp with their women seeing them off. 5US and inset 5USa

President Wilson named Pershing as commander-in-chief, a post he retained for the duration. Pershing, who was a major general, was promoted to full general in the National Army, and was made responsible for the organization, training, and supply of a combined professional and draft Army and National Guard force that eventually grew from 27,000 inexperienced men to two Armies totalling over two million soldiers.

Left: In cold, wet conditions on campaign. 3USa

Above: On horseback in Mexico, leading the hunt for the revolutionary leader Pancho Villa, Pershing leads his command across a river. 3US

Major General Wood addressing trainee officers at Fort McPherson, First Officers' Training Camp, Plattsburg.
6US
Making officers in just three months presented a challenge. A Regular officer lectures officer cadets. 7USa

Student officers at Fort Myer Training Camp. 7US

Trainee officers on a route march; The man without a hat is Louis Swift the son of a millionaire. WWI/US003

Major Theodore Roosevelt leading a company of officer candidates to mess at first Plattsburg training camp. Major Roosevelt fought in France with the First Division, was wounded, decorated, and came home a lieutenant colonel. He entered politics and became Governor-General of the Philippines in 1932. With the onset of the Second World War he returned to active duty and was given command of the 26th Infantry Regiment, 1st Infantry Division. Roosevelt saw action in North Africa, Sicily and commanded Allied Forces in Sardinia and on the Italian mainland. He was the chief liaison officer to the French Army in Italy for General Dwight D. Eisenhower. Despite a heart condition and arthritis that forced him to use a cane, General Roosevelt led the assault on Utah Beach, landing with the first wave of troops. He died in France less than a month later of a heart attack. 7US

Dubbed 'America's biggest lottery'. A blind-folded Secretary of State in Washington drew out a number, and every man in the 4,577 selective draft districts in the United States holding that particular number was the first man drawn to the colours in his district. As the numbers were drawn lists were posted throughout the country.

Right: Men in New York searched the lists daily. 8US

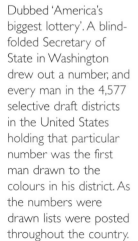

Chicago draft men marching up Michigan Avenue before cheering crowds. This helped them to feel that the nation was behind their sacrifice. IOUS

Camps were not finished when the first draft quotas turned up. Drills began at once among the clutter and confusion of building operations. 9USa

Draft 'rookies' from New York, after their first meal in camp, are introduced to the novelty of cleaning their mess tins in building sand. 9USb

There was a woeful lack of uniforms and these men from Cincinnati carry out their first drills in the civvies they wore from home. 9USc

In this remarkable group scene caught by a newspaper cameraman at the Union Station in Kansas City, we are presented with an image that tells better than a thousand words the anguish and tragedy brought to millions of American families as loved ones parted. We are informed that this man refused to claim exemption from military service, although he was entitled to do so. Likely some influence could have been brought to bear in his case so as to avoid the draft, as wealth and possible position in the community is in evidence by the fox furs, ring and wristwatch. 11US

Draft men at a Texas camp have just drawn their kit and are wearing their uniforms for the first time. 9USd

Target practice shooting on the firing range at Camp Grant. All communications from France laid emphasis on the need to develop skills in shooting; especially those coming from General Pershing. 14USa

Bayonet practice under a hot July sun in Texas. They are wearing gas masks to simulate war conditions. 14USb

'Over the Top!' at Fort Foote. 14USc

A regiment of the 28th Infantry Division at Camp Hancock. A leader-directed group carry out calisthenics as a form of synchronized physical training. This was usually customized by a call and response routine, the purpose being to increase group cohesion and discipline. I2US

Review of the 53rd Field Artillery Brigade, 28th Division, at Camp Hancock. The full complement of an artillery brigade comprises 208 officers and 4,769 men with 3,883 horses (including some mules).
13US

These soldiers are marching to the ferry boats at Alpine Landing, New Jersey, that will carry them to the transport at Hoboken. In the background is Blackledge-Kearney House, believed at one time to be the headquarters of British General Cornwallis in November 1776, during the War of Independence. This picture was withheld during the First World War as it showed a place of embarkation. 15US

The first leg of their journey to France; the ferryboat is transporting these men to the docks at Hoboken where transports await them.

Inset: Soldiers are being handed Safe Arrival postcards which they could address to their next of kin informing them of their safe arrival in Europe. These were collected and mailed upon a cable being received that the transports had arrived safely.
WWI/US004

The Yanks Are Coming

DURING the nineteen months of war more than 2,000,000 American soldiers were transported to France. Half a million of these went over in the first thirteen months, and a further million and a half in the final six months. Most of the troops who sailed for Europe left from New York, half landing in France and half in England after a journey lasting sixteen days.

Major General David C. Shanks oversaw troop movements from Hoboken. Over 1,656,000 men were expedited from that port. 16USa

Hoboken, July 1918, soldiers boarding the *Leviathan* which could transport 12,000 men at a time – the equivalent of a German division. 16US

The Yanks are Coming. In this line of transports are the *George Washington* and the *America* steaming as all lines do – majestically – towards the continent of Europe. 18US

The caption for this: 'The Great Adventure'. WWIUS005

Above: Attention is being directed to anti U-boat precautions. WW1US007a.

Signalling from an escort destroyer 17USa

C DECK
THROW NOTHING
OVERBOARD.
FLOATING ARTICLES REVEAL
OUR COURSE TO ENEMY
SUBMARINES

The destroyer *Henderson* zigzagging and making smoke to mask the convoy during a submarine alert. 20USa

A convoy under escort from a 'Blimp' – a dirigible – on the lookout for tell-tale wash of a submarine periscope. 20USb

Scanning the sea from the bridge of a destroyer. Owing to the vigilance of the navy not one east-bound American transport was torpedoed by the German Navy. 20USb

From aboard USS *Whipple* – stages in destroying a U-boat: periscope sighted; rolling depth charges and blown to the surface. 20US; 19USa; 19USb; 19US

The French west coast seaport of Brett. It was here that 791,000 Yankee soldiers first set foot on French soil. 21US

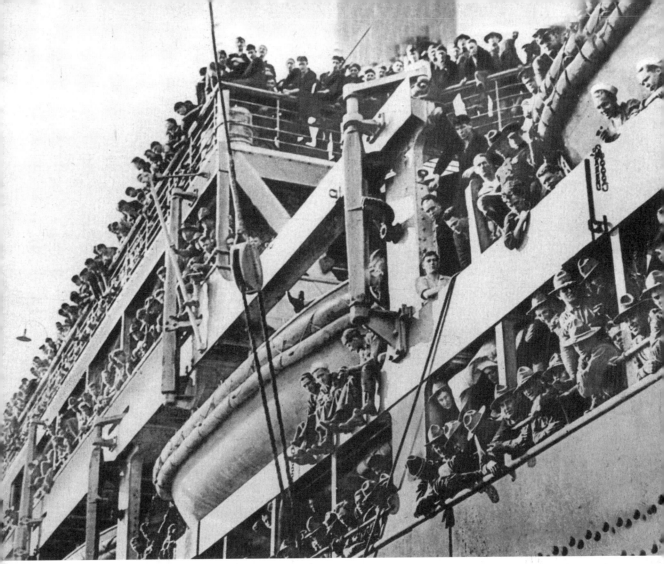

'So this is France!' Americans getting their first view of the soil they had sailed 3,000 miles to fight on. The Leviathan, carrying 12,000 troops and 4,000 sailors, 200 Red Cross nurses and 700 casual officers was coming to anchor in the busy harbour of Brett when this picture was taken. An hour before, the huge transport had been attacked by a pack of U-boats and had successfully fought them off with stern guns and assistance from destroyers. 22US

Opposite: French civilians gathered to welcome the first arrivals: 'Les Yankees sont arrives! Vivent les Yankees!' Played off the ship by an American military band. Debarkation of the 42nd (Rainbow) Division at St Nazaire. This famous division, made up of National Guardsmen from twenty-seven states and the District of Columbia, landed its headquarters at St Nazaire 1 November 1917. Other contingents landed at St Nazaire, Brett and Liverpool from 1 November to 7 December. 23US WW1?US008

Fifth US Marines en route to training area, June 1917. Their first ride in the famous French railway wagons which carried the signs 'Hommes 40, Chevaux 8' (40 men or 8 horses), and provided the basis for many a joke launched by men of the British Empire, and now by men of the American Expeditionary Force. 32US

Invasion! The Thirteenth Engineers (Chicago) crossing Westminster Bridge 15 August 1917. The first armed force of a foreign power to march in England's capital since William the Conqueror in 1066. Also in this parade were the Eleventh Engineers (New York) and the Fifteenth (Pittsburg).

Inset: General Pershing after landing at Liverpool 8 June 1917. 34US

Pershing arrives in France. The general and his staff on the deck of a Channel steamer are welcomed by the French civil and military dignitaries at the port of Boulogne 13 June 1917. 24USa

A guard of honour greets Pershing at Boulogne railway station where the American commander boarded a train for Paris. 25US

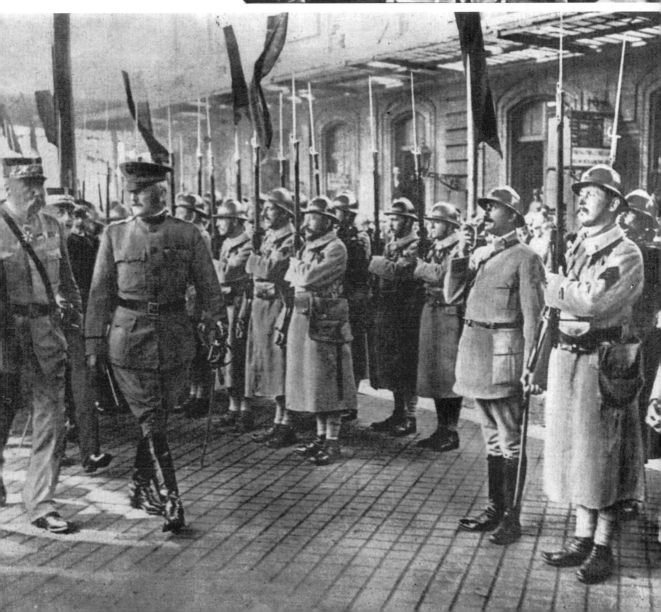

Time to honour a joint hero of France and America Paul Yves Roch Gilbert du Motier, Marquis de La Fayette. In the American War of Independence Lafayette served as a major-general in the Continental Army under George Washington. On the 4 July 1917 a Colour Guard comprising men of the 2nd Battalion, 16th Infantry Division, took part in the honouring of the patriot. Commenting on the standard of drill one Frenchman is reported to have said:

'Orders are promptly executed, manoeuvers are effected with skill, everyone knows his place and his business. The operations of disembarking, gathering the small units and marching to the barracks are carried out with discipline and order. The men are well set up and seem perfectly at ease on French soil. With their khaki uniforms closer cut than those of the English, with their picturesque sombreros and their eminently practical equipment they give the impression of cohesion. The soldiers appear to be strong, athletic and healthy, and one has the feeling that the nerves of such a troop will act with force and precision at the hour of combat.'

WWI/US009

Training and Trench Fighting

THE FUNDAMENTAL doctrine insisted upon by General Pershing is found in his statement of the general principles governing the training of units of the American Expeditionary Forces:

'The methods to be employed must remain or become distinctly our own. The general principles governing combat remain unchanged in their essence. This war has developed special features which involve special phases of training, but the fundamental ideas enunciated in our Drill Regulations, Small Arms Firing Manual, Field Service Regulations and other service manuals remain the guide for both officers and soldiers and constitute the standard by which their efficiency is to be measured, except as modified in detail by instructions from these headquarters.

'The rifle and the bayonet are the principal weapons of the infantry soldier. He will be trained to a high degree of skill as a marksman both on the target range and in field firing. An aggressive spirit must be developed until the soldier feels himself, as a bayonet fighter, invincible in battle.'

Arriving divisions were to be sent to a training area (the artillery to one of the special camps) for a period of one to two months. During that period the division would be equipped, receive special training and become acclimated in the atmosphere of war.

The welcoming parades are over, now it is time to get down to business. General Pershing at his desk at 31 Rue Constantine, Paris. 25US

American marines wearing French Adrian helmets practice throwing bombs. 30aUS

The French soldier with five stripes on his arm indicating the experience available to instruct the Americans. 30US

Major General Blacklock (left) and Brigadier General A. G. Hubback look on as the Americans undergo training. 29aUS

Officers and NCOs of a
Highland regiment oversee
the training of the
newcomers. 31USa

British officers giving
instruction on the Vickers
machine gun. 29USc

Former Yank, Sergeant Harris, who once served in the 1st Regiment
New Mexico National Guard, now with the AEF helps them get the
hang of the Vickers. 29USb

General Headquarters of the American Expeditionary Force at Chaumont. 33US

Right: In the Toul sector where the 1st Division took over the first trenches to be held by Americans. 35USa

Taking a look at Jerry. Officers and men of the 18th Infantry, 1st Division in the front line at Ansauville. 36US

The French designed and built 75mm field gun which fired the first shot at the Germans on behalf of the United States of America, and was crewed by men of Battery C, 6th Field Artillery, 1st Division. It was fired at 0600hrs, 23 October 1917. 37US

Here lie the first soldiers of the United States to fall on the soil of France for liberty and justice. The inscriptions on the graves of Corporal James D. Gresham, Private Thomas F. Enright, and Merle D. Hay, 16th Infantry, 1st Division. They were killed on the night of 3 November 1917 when a German patrol raided the trenches near Bures, Bathelemont. 39US

An early casualty. 40USa

A Young Mens Christian Association worker serving hot chocolate to Yanks and Poilus in the Front Line. 38US

Visit by the American Secretary of State for War Newton Baker to the Luneville Sector of trenches, 19 March 1918. 42US

The first German prisoner to be captured by the 26th Division is proudly paraded for the camera by Sergeant John Letzing, 104th Infantry. The prisoner's name was Robert Froehlich and he was taken on 17 February 1918.

Yanks and Poilus behind the Front Line drink a toast to the Allies. 39USXb

Miss Gladys McIntyre of the Salvation Army serving doughnuts to the men of the 26th Division. 39USXc

Men of the 167th Infantry (4th Alabama) eating chow in the Front Line trenches. 40USXa

Men of the 165th Infantry (69th New York National Guard) about to move up to the Front Line at Croismare, 2 March 1918. 40USXb

Among the first of many: Private Dyer J. Bird, 166th Infantry, at Domjevin, 3 March 1918. Private Bird was killed at a listening post when a German patrol attacked it. The coffin is a luxury, but the image would have been good for those back in the States. 40USXd

A 42nd Division outpost in the woods of Parroy, east of Luneville, 5 March 1918. The 42nd Division was serving with the French VII Corps. A few moments after this picture was taken the position was blown up by a German shell. 44US

Intelligence officers of the 42nd Division interrogating prisoners captured at Baccarat. 43USa

Men of the 26th Field Signal Battalion engaged in phone installation in the Soissons sector 12 March 1918. 43US

Intelligence personnel of the 168th Infantry at Badonviller, trying on snipers' specially designed camouflage gear developed by the British. 46USa

Men of the 167th Infantry resting behind the lines near Neuviller, 10 May 1918.
46USb

The 150th Field Artillery in action near St Pole.
WWI/US010

Before going into battle men of the 101st Infantry attend communion in a cave near Chemin des Dames. The warriors are thus encouraged to enter the fray believing in the rightness of the cause, and that the Almighty favours the Allies. 45US

Chapter Four

First Offensive
Action – Cantigny

CONCERNING THE FIRST OFFENSIVE action carried out by the AEF one commentator of the day expressed the following:

> 'The value to the allied cause of the success at Cantigny was entirely out of proportion to its strategic importance. At this period never during the entire war were the Allies more disheartened. And now the future depended upon the American soldier. Would he win against the experienced and confident enemy then in the midst of astonishing successes? The measure of United States troops was to be taken. The discouraged Allies, then on the defensive, waited in alternate hope and doubt.'

To the US 28th Division was given the task of undertaking the first offensive in the organized offensive operation by American troops. On 25 April 1918 the First Division took over the active Cantigny sector near Montdidier. Strategically, Cantigny was not important, but it marked a salient in one of the most advanced parts of the German lines. It was desirable to straighten the line in that sector, especially in view of an allied offensive which was being contemplated. However, that offensive had to be given

General Pershing addresses officers of the 1st Division – the first American division to enter an active battle sector in Europe, 16 April 1918. Six weeks later they were in action at Cantigny. WWI/US011

French children take time from their school lessons to greet the advance unit of the American 101st Ammunition Train, Soulosse 10 April 1918. 48US

up owing to the development of the third German drive on 27 May 1918. Nevertheless, the plans for the capture of Cantigny were carried out, partly for the local advantage, but chiefly for demonstrating American troops in an independent offensive action.

After the war Major General E. F. McGlachlin, Jr. commanding general of the US 1st Division in the Allied Army of Occupation described the action for the Official History:

The 28th Infantry attacked Cantigny at 0645hrs on 28 May, 1918, after violent artillery preparation of one hour. The regiment advanced in three lines. The first line closed in to within forty to fifty yards of the barrage, the troops advancing in conformity to the barrage, which progressed at the rate of 100 yards in two minutes. The second line rapidly closed on the first line in order that all elements would be 200 yards from the old front line at H plus 10 minutes. This was done to lessen casualties should an enemy's barrage be put down. The third line conformed to the advance. The objective was reached as per schedule at 0720hrs. Patrols were immediately pushed forward and automatic rifle posts were established in shell holes on the line of surveillance to cover the consolidation.

'We have passed successfully the most terrific test ever imposed on American troops in France and we have proved that American militia can be relied upon to fight to the death under orders.'
Colonel John H. Parker
102nd Infantry Division

The village of Seicheprey. On 20 April it was the scene of the first serious encounter between the Americans and the Germans. The German assaulting troops amounted to 2,800 men, which included in the lead a battalion of *Stosstruppen,* especially trained and carefully rehearsed. The attack was met by elements of 102nd Infantry Division under the command of Colonel John H. Parker (opposite top left). The assaulting Germans lost 1,851 with the defending Americans losing 1,064. 47US

The second line, which advanced, consolidated with a line of trenches and wired the line of resistance. The third line, on its arrival, began the consolidation of three strong points, one about 200 yards east of the chateau in CANTIGNY; the second in the woods at the north-eastern exit of CANTIGNY, and the third at the cemetery just north of CANTIGNY. D Company, of the 1st Engineers supervised the consolidation of these strong points, and the lines of surveillance and resistance.

Throughout, the attack progressed with slight resistance and with practically no reaction on the part of the enemy artillery. The section of French flame-throwers proved invaluable in cleaning up the town of CANTIGNY and driving the enemy out of dugouts. During the cleaning up of CANTIGNY our troops were engaged in minor fights, but for the most part the objective was gained with rapidity and with considerable ease. Not before noon did the enemy artillery and machine-gun fire become heavy. From this time on and during the seventy-two hours following, the positions about CANTIGNY were heavily shelled, both by large and by small calibre guns. Enemy machine-gun fire was also heavy.

At 0730hrs, a small enemy infantry counter-attack was reported to have been delivered without success against the BOIS FONTAINE. At 1710hrs the enemy launched another small infantry counter-attack from the western tip of the BOIS FRAMICOURT. This was broken up by our artillery. The attack was followed at 1845hrs, after a heavy preparation and barrage fire, by enemy infantry advancing in several waves from the southern and western edges of the BOIS FRAMICOURT. The first wave succeeded in getting through before our barrage was put down. It was driven back by infantry fire and the following waves were smothered by artillery fire. During the night of 28 May the two companies of the 18th Infantry Regiment in reserve, were ordered into the operation to support the 28th Infantry. One

Air view of the Battle of Cantingy. 49US Pershing reported to the Secretary of War: 'On the morning of 28 May the First Division attacked the German positions on its front, taking with splendid dash the town of Cantigny and all other objectives which were organized and held steadfastly against vicious counter-attacks and galling artillery fire.' WWI/US012

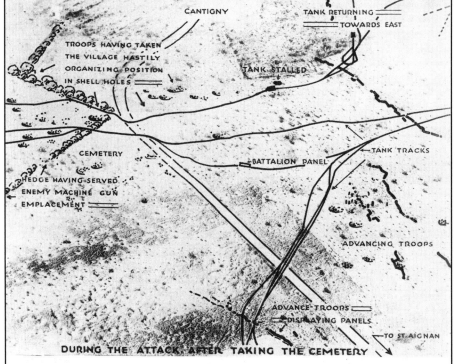

CANTIGNY

TROOPS HAVING TAKEN
THE VILLAGE HASTILY
ORGANIZING POSITION
IN SHELL HOLES

TANK RETURNING
TOWARDS EAST

TANK STALLED

CEMETERY

BATTALION PANEL

TANK TRACKS

HEDGE HAVING SERVED
ENEMY MACHINE GUN
EMPLACEMENT

ADVANCING TROOPS

ADVANCE TROOPS
DISPLAYING PANELS

TO ST. AIGNAN

DURING THE ATTACK AFTER TAKING THE CEMETERY

The jump off at Cantigny. After a violent artillery preparation of one hour the 28th Infantry Regiment, with Colonel Hanson E. Ely in command, began the attack at 0645hrs, 28 May. The objective was taken as planned at 0720hrs. 50US

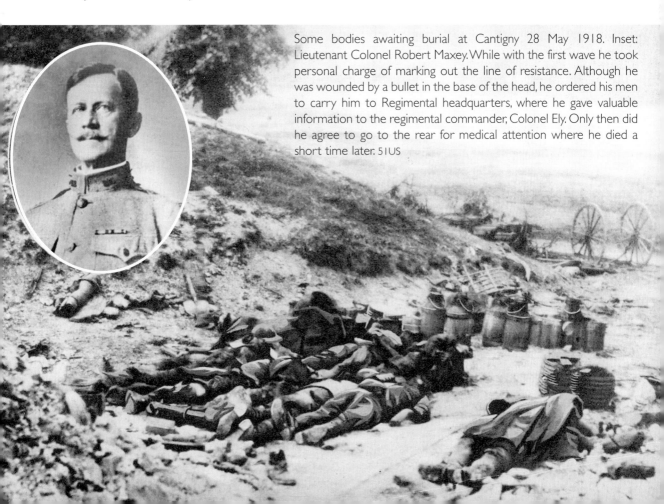

Some bodies awaiting burial at Cantigny 28 May 1918. Inset: Lieutenant Colonel Robert Maxey. While with the first wave he took personal charge of marking out the line of resistance. Although he was wounded by a bullet in the base of the head, he ordered his men to carry him to Regimental headquarters, where he gave valuable information to the regimental commander, Colonel Ely. Only then did he agree to go to the rear for medical attention where he died a short time later. 51US

battalion of the 18th Infantry Regiment, in the vicinity of VILLERS-TOURNELLE was ordered to take position in rear of the south-west corner of the BOIS DES GLANDS.

29 MAY

Between 0600hrs, and 0700hrs am, the enemy launched two small counter-attacks which were quickly broken up by artillery. At 1745hrs, the enemy launched its second heavy counter-attack. On the left elements of the 28th Infantry Regiment drew back slightly, but the remainder of the line withstood the attack. Artillery and infantry fire broke up this assault.

30 MAY

At 0530hrs the enemy made his final counter-attack. It was preceded by a barrage and heavy preparation fire. The enemy attacked in two waves from the LALVAL wood. This attack was also broken up by rifle, machine gun and artillery fire. In all, seven enemy counter-attacks were reported as being launched. Three of these attacks appeared to have been made by at least a battalion of infantry. The first was the most determined and fell principally on the centre battalion, and the right of the left battalion, and was preceded by a preparation fire of 210mm and 150mm projectiles and then a barrage of 150mm and 77mm shells. The enemy followed this barrage from 125 to 200 yards thus enabling our troops to be in full readiness after the barrage had passed them.

After the morning of 30 May, enemy activity lessened. This enabled a greater part of the 28th Infantry Regiment to be relieved by the 16th Infantry Regiment on the night of 30-31 May. The following night the remainder of the regiment was relieved and the command of the sector passed to the Commanding Officer 16th Infantry.

Second Lieutenant Daniel Willard, 102nd Field Artillery being awarded the Croix de Guerre for conspicuous bravery, Manoncourt, France, 11 June 1918. WWI/US013

Scenes in the wrecked village of Cantigny after it had been captured by the Americans.

Top left: Brought in on a handcart, Private Barnes 'takes it philosophically'. 52USb

Above: German prisoners taken at Cantigny being searched. 52USa

Left: German soldier killed during fighting in the village 28 May. 52USd

Below: 28th Infantry Division Dressing Station in the village of Cantigny treating German wounded. 53USa

Prisoners captured at Cantigny marching through Le Mesnil-St Firmin, 28 May 1918. 53US

Ambulances roll into Paris to American Military Hospital Number One. 55US

Chapter Five

Chateau Thierry

ON 27 MAY THE GERMANS launched their Aisne-Marne offensive. Success during the first days of their assault was more marked than anything that German arms had yet secured. Paris had already been subjected to long-range bombardment and violent air raids, and now the state of morale of that capital may be judged by the estimated one million plus people who left Paris during May and June 1918.

Brigadier-General Fox Conner, Chief G-3, Operations Division General Staff), General Headquarters, American Expeditionary Force, prepared the notes on the German May offensives and the Allied counter-attack in July 1918.

On 1 June, just when the future seemed darkest, the 2nd American Division, which had been moved from around Verdun–St. Mihiel, was thrown across the Chateau Thierry – Paris road. The German thrust toward Paris was stopped.

At the same time, elements of the 3rd Division were placed along the River Marne together with various bodies of French troops; wherever soldiers of the 3rd Division were in the defence line, there too the German advance stopped.

By 30 June the Germans realized that the arrival of American soldiers at the front might soon turn the tide in favour of the Allies. By that date some 900,000 Americans were on French soil, and this was just the beginning. Now having no illusions as to the impact American troops must have on the outcome of the conflict, the Germans decided to try one final effort to obtain a decision in their favour. The final German attack was accordingly launched in the Champagne on 15 July.

On that date the disposition of the American divisions in France was as follows: The 32nd, 35th, 5th and 77th Divisions were along a line between the Swiss border and Luneville. The 82nd was in line north of Toul. The four regiments of the 93rd Division were with the French in line between the Argonne and the Meuse. The 42nd was in reserve to meet the expected German attack in Champagne. The 3rd and 26th were in line in the region of Chateau Thierry, and the 28th had elements with the American and French units in the same region. The 2nd and 4th were in reserve near Meaux, and the 1st near Beauvais ready for use in the planned counter-attack. The 27th and 30th were in line with the British near Ypres. The 33rd, 78th and 80th were completing their training with the British, the 91st had just arrived at Le Havre and the 79th was arriving at Brest. The 29th, 37th, 83rd, 89th 90th and 92nd were in training areas around Chaumont.

The Allies knew the area where the Germans would attack. In the first days of July 1918, it became apparent that the Germans would be unable to launch more than one other great attack, and towards the 10th of the month it was believed certain that if the enemy attacked, the blow would fall in Champagne. Thanks to the arrival of American troops, the Allied reserves were now sufficiently numerous to justify a counter-attack, and if the Champagne front could hold with the troops already allotted to it, the Allied Command retained complete freedom in the selection of the front upon which the counter-attack should fall.

The approach by the German lines along the Marne toward Paris had caused apprehension throughout France; it was essential that the threat on Paris be relieved at the earliest. Aside from reasons of morale, purely material reasons also demanded the reduction of the Marne salient as the first task of the Allies when the initiative should pass to their hands. Paris contained a multitude of essential war industries, and so long as the Germans maintained their lines, these industries were seriously hampered by the constant long range bombardments and air raids. The

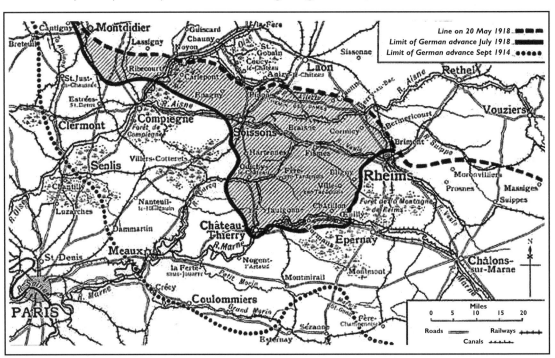

Stemming the tide at Chateau Thierry. The Germans began their offensive between the Aisne and the Marne 27 May 1918, and the US 3rd Division was placed at the disposal of the French. The first unit to enter the line was the 7th Machine Gun Battalion which put up a stubborn resistance at Chateau Thierry, preventing the Germans from crossing the River Marne. 60US

great east and west railroad through Chateau-Thierry had to be regained by the Allies as a first necessity in the troop movements required in any general offensive.

The general plan for the Allied counter-attack of 18 July involved attacking the entire west face of the Marne salient. This main attack was at first to pivot on Chateau-Thierry; later the Allies in the region of Chateau-Thierry were to take up the attack. The Allies were also to attack that part of the German salient south of

German artillery shelling the rear of the American lines at Chateau-Thierry in an attempt to prevent reinforcements coming up. WWI/US015a

Chateau Thierry – forever to be associated with American military involvement in Europe. North is to the top and the Germans reached the north bank of the Marne river; centre is the Marie, square and road – Rue Carnot – leading to the Marne bridge, which had been destroyed. The Americans were in the buildings on the opposite side of the river. 59US

the Marne and to the south-west of Rheims. The plan required attacking the entire Marne salient, the principal blow falling at first on the west face, with the critical point at which eventual success or failure would be determined, south-west of Soissons.

The three divisions selected to break the most sensitive part of the German line were the 2nd American, the 1st Moroccan (French), and the 1st American. If these three divisions could seize and hold the heights south of Soissons, the salient proper would become untenable and its ultimate reduction was assured.

At 0435hrs, 18 July, after some of the American infantry had moved at double time into the line, and when some of their artillery had just moved into position, the 1st and 2nd American Divisions and the 1st Moroccan Division jumped off. The

Infantry about to move up to the Marne at Chateau-Thierry where the Germans are threatening to break through for an advance on Paris. WWI/US015b

The Germans were stopped when they reached this point of the north bank at the rubble of the destroyed bridge. WWI/US016a

Some of the men who stopped them; soldiers of the 9th Machine Gun Battalion, 3rd Division. WWI/US016

The town of Vaux as elements of the 9th and 23rd Infantry Regiments, 2nd Division, entered the streets 1 July 1918. It had been subjected to heavy shelling by the Americans and dead Germans can be seen lying in the street. Targets for the guns had been pinpointed by a French stonemason who had previously lived in the town. 65US

Germans were driven back, and the results upon which ultimate success depended were secured. The 2nd Division advanced 8km in the first twenty-six hours, took about 3,000 prisoners, two batteries of 150mm guns, sixty-six light guns and 15.000 rounds of 77mm ammunition. This division suffered some 4,000 casualties and, as it had made exhausting marches to reach the battlefield, and having recently been withdrawn from its desperate fighting at Chateau-Thierry, the division was relieved after the second day.

The 1st Division suffered 7,000 casualties, of whom it is believed that not one was a prisoner. Sixty per cent of its infantry officers were killed or wounded. In the 16th

Men of Company B, 166th Infantry Regiment, (4th Ohio Infantry) entering La Ferte-sous-Jouarre, 23 July 1918. 68US

The drive is on to push the Germans out of the Marne salient. Wagons of the 150th Field Artillery (1st Regiment Indiana Field Artillery) passing through Chateau Thierry, 25 July 1918. 69US

and 18th Infantry Regiments all field officers were casualties except the colonels, and in the 26th Infantry Regiment all field officers, including the colonels, were casualties. Notwithstanding its losses, the 1st Division, by constant attacks throughout four days and nights, had broken through the entrenchments in the German pivot to a depth of 11km. They had captured sixty-eight field guns and quantities of other material, in addition to 3,500 prisoners taken from the seven separate German divisions which had been thrown against the 1st United States Division in the enemy's desperate effort to hold ground, which was essential to his retaining the Marne salient.

While the work of the 1st and 2nd Divisions attracted most attention because

Chateau Thierry when the Americans crossed the Marne to march on to St Mihiel. 82US

Men of the 111th Infantry Regiment, 28th Division, at Chateau Thierry on their way to take part in the counter-offensive. 82US

These Americans, men of the 1st Division, appear to bitterly resent the presence of the Signal Corps photographer. They are about to go into the line to relieve a brigade of French Moroccans near Coeuvres-et-Valsery. On 18 July, the day after they took up their position, they were thrown into an attack on Berzy-le-Sec and the heights above Soissons. After four days constant fighting they had advanced 11km and taken 3,500 prisoners. 65US

A sunken road littered with dead Germans killed during desperate fighting with the 16th Infantry Regiment in its attack on Missy-au-Bois. 66US

Coming to close quarters with the enemy; these men of the 166th Infantry Regiment check farm buildings at Villers-sur-Fere. 70US

Men of the 103rd Infantry Regiment, 26th Division, going into the attack at dawn 18 July 1918. These men reached their objective, the village of Torcy, in thirty-five minutes. 67US

of the special importance of their attack, they were not the only American divisions to participate in the 18 July offensive. A little to the south of the 2nd Division the 4th Division was in line with the French, and the 4th Division joined in the attack and continued to advance until 22 July when it relieved the 42nd Division on 2nd August. The 26th Division was just north-west of Chateau-Thierry and together with the 167th French Division formed the 1st American Corps, which was the first American corps to exercise tactical command. This corps acted as a pivot in the beginning and later had to advance under difficult conditions. Notwithstanding the difficult nature of its task, and the fact that it lost 5,300 officers and men, the 26th remained in the

German dead at Mezy 21 July 1918. 73US

attack until 25 July; some of its elements having been continuously fighting for eight days and nights. The division had advanced more than 17km against determined enemy resistance, had taken the villages of Torcy, Belleau, Givry, Epieds, and Trugny, and had captured large quantities of enemy materiel. On 25-26 July, the 26th Division was relieved by the 42nd Division, which, after having taken some part in the successful resistance to the German attack of 15 July in Champagne, had been brought round to the Chateau-Thierry region.

Brigadier-General Douglas MacArthur commanding 84 Brigade, seen here at his temporary headquarters near Fresnes. He went on to make his military reputation in the Second World War and Korean War. WWI/US017

East of Chateau-Thierry, and south of the Marne, the 3rd Division had broken up all efforts made against it on 15 July. Now, on 20 July, the 3rd Division received orders to join in the counter-attack. By skillful work of the command and staff, the division had gotten well across the Marne by the 22nd and without having encountered serious resistance. From the 22nd to 25th the division was engaged in bitter fighting in the wooded slopes leading up to the village of le Charmel, which was taken on the evening of 25 July. Constantly fighting its way forward the division took Roncheres; and finally on 30 July was relieved by the 32nd Division, after having suffered a total loss of 7,900.

The next day the 42nd Division attacked, and by the 28 July it had crossed the *Ourcq* and taken Sergy. Here the enemy offered desperate resistance, launching counter-attack after counter-attack, the village of Sergy changing hands four times. But the 42nd definitely occupied Sergy on the morning of 29 July and continued to

American fallen of the 38th Infantry Regiment, killed in the hand-to-hand fighting at Merzy. 73USa

The burial party. 81US

Troops of the 2nd Battalion, 126th Infantry Regiment, assembling in a wheat field preparatory to an attack near Coutmont. WWI/US018a

Men of the 2nd Battalion, 126th Infantry Regiment (Michigan National Guard), assembling for the attack at Coutmont, 1 August 1918. WWI/US018b

press forward until 2 August when the enemy withdrew. The 4th Division now relieved the 42nd and on 6 August, the operation of the reduction of the Marne salient terminated and the battlefront stabilized on the line of the River *Vesle*.

The 2nd and 3rd Divisions had played a conspicuous part in stopping the

Germans killed at Cierges, in a bayonet charge by men of the 125th Infantry Regiment. WWI/US018

Headquarters of 58th Infantry Regiment at Chery-Chartreuve Farm, 9 August 1918. 74US

French tanks, Renault FT-17, moving through infantry of the 32nd Division, to support French units operating on the American left flank. 78US

Men of Company K, 128th Infantry Regiment, 32nd Division, in line on Valpries farm in front of Juvigny, 29 August 1918. In three days these men and their comrades of the Wisconsin-Michigan division put to rout five German divisions; the *7th, 7th Reserve, 223nd, 237th* and *238th*. In the last days of August, Major General Haan's 32nd Division went into line with General Mangin's 10th French Army in front of the strongly fortified German position on the Juvigny plateau north of Soissons. The 32nd Division formed the spearhead of the attack with Juvigny, the key position, as its objective. Terrific fighting ensued. On the third day a determined manoeuvre enabled the 32nd Division to take Juvigny and the plateau beyond. General Mangin cited the division later; 'for the brilliant conduct and splendid courage it displayed in taking the town of Juvigny, the memory of which will remain forever intact with us and which will place in history the glorious deeds of the 32nd Division and of its able and valiant chief, General Haan.' The men in the picture are only 300 yards from the crest, which is the middle of No Man's Land between the two forces, about three kilometres west of Juvigny, captured the next day by General Haan's division. General Haan was present when this picture was taken. 79US

German advance on Paris. Eight American divisions (the 1st, 2nd, 3rd, 4th, 26th, 28th, 32nd and 42nd) had played a major role in the reduction of the Marne salient. Total American casualties were over 30,000. The initiative would pass into Allied hands and the Commander-in-Chief would now turn his attention to St. Mihiel.

Kneeling behind hastily constructed shelters these soldiers of the 167th Infantry Regiment take on the counter-attacking Germans. 72US

A priority target for the American infantryman – these two Germans with a flame-thrower. 79USXa

Dead of the 167th Infantry Regiment (Alabama) litter the field behind the advance on Fere-en-Tardenois. Note the rifles stuck in the ground to indicate a fatality to the gravediggers. 71USa

St Mihiel

THE GERMAN OFFENSIVE of 21 March 1918 and the succeeding offensives had postponed the planned formation of an American army responsible for its own sector in Europe. From 27 May, American divisions were committed to saving Paris and in reducing the Marne salient created by the German advance. It was fully intended that the original purpose be returned to as soon as the crisis was over.

On 24 July a conference between the American, British and French Commanders-in-Chief and Marshal Foch was held at Bombon. The conference agreed that all the Allied forces should pass to an offensive attitude, and definite operations were agreed upon as follows:

(a) Continuation of the reduction of the Marne salient: to secure as a minimum result the release of the Paris-Chalons railroad.

(b) Reduction of the Amiens salient thus securing the release of the Paris-Amiens railroad.

(c) Reduction of the St. Mihiel salient.

(d) Release of the coal mining regions in the north [area of Bethune] and driving the enemy away from the ports of Dunkerque and Calais.

American front line observation post at Les Eparges, looking out across No Man's Land two days before the battle began for the reduction of the St. Mihiel salient. The 26th Division would cross this ground in the forthcoming attack. 91US

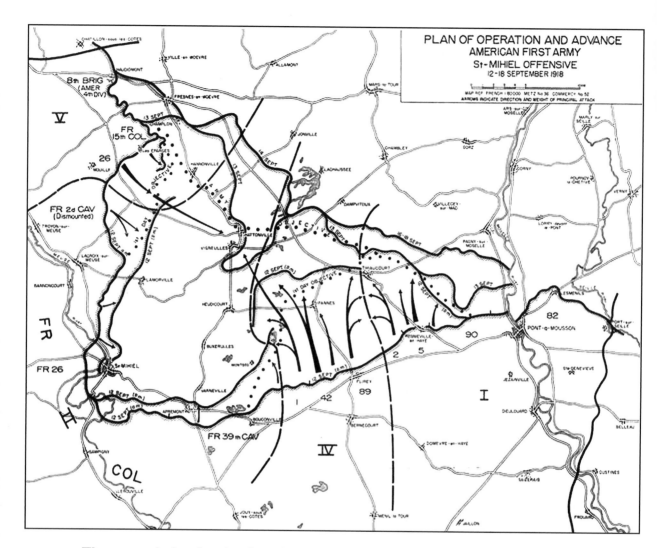

The general plan for the American Fourth Army assault:

(a) An attack from the south through the wooded country south-east of Vigneulles.

(b) A follow-up attack on the southern flank of the main effort in the south.

(c) An attack from the west over the eastern heights of the Meuse between Les Eparges and Seuzey toward Hannonville and Hattonville.

(d) An exploitation and follow-up attack on the right flank of the western attack.

(e) Exploitation of gains.

The reduction of the St. Mihiel salient was made the task of the American army, but no approximate date for this effort was fixed. However, it was agreed on 24 July to begin troop movements which would finally result in the formation, in the Chateau-Thierry region, of an American army of two army corps of three divisions each.

The offensive value of the salient to the Germans lay in the fact that it interrupted French communications from west to east on the main railroad Paris-Nancy, while constantly threatening the entire region between Nancy and Bar-le-Duc, as well as that between Bar-le-Duc and Verdun. The principal defensive value of the salient from the German point of view, was that it covered the strategic centre of Metz and the Briey iron basin. It must be reduced before any general offensive against these two vital points, or even further east, could be contemplated.

Naturally the French Command had studied the question of the reduction of the salient, but the one attempt made in 1915 had failed, and the general situation had stopped further French attempts.

Various considerations dictated the occupation of this part of the line by the American army when it arrived in force. Consequently the reduction of the St.

'We ought to have that mountain' were the words of General Pershing when he first viewed Mont Sec; towering 380 metres above the Woevre lowland. From Mont Sec, which the Germans were holding in strength, they had dominated the entire St. Mihiel salient for four years. It took the American Fourth Army just over a day to capture the lot. During the battle the 1st Division simply smothered Mont Sec with smoke and went round it. Brigadier-General F. E. Bamford, 2 Brigade, 1st Division is seen here scanning the ground. 83US

This is a photograph showing the top of Mont Sec with Fort du Camp des Romains dominating all sides. This was taken by the US Air Services during its occupation by the Germans. 84USa

General Philippe Pétain.

Mihiel salient was studied by the American Command as the first large-scale operation by an American army. However, the Allied success in August caused the Allied High Command to decide on a combined offensive late in September, in which the American army should attack west of the Meuse. Several conferences were held between the Commander-in-Chief Marshal Foch and General Pétain, which resulted in limiting the St. Mihiel operation with the line Regnieville-en-Haye Thiaucourt—Vigneulles as the objective. A definite decision was taken on 9

Marshal Ferdinand Foch.

Fort Camp des Romains dominated the tip of the German salient; seen here during occupation by the Germans. 84USb

Dugouts housing some of the 89th Division prior to the battle of St. Mihiel. Within the salient the Germans had built more pretentious dwellings of concrete. Some German officers' quarters contained bathrooms, and had flower gardens at the front. 87US

August to unite at least a part of the American forces who found their divisions spread from Switzerland to the English Channel. In addition to divisions, large numbers of troops such as artillery, aviation, tank corps and services of all kinds had to be found, and concentrated for the operation. The total of troops amounted to approximately 600,000. The necessity for concentrating these troops in a clandestine manner, so to secure at least a tactical surprise, added to the difficulties and required long night marches. Still another difficulty lay in the fact that, due to necessities arising from the successes obtained by the enemy in March and April, America had shipped over infantry in advance of auxiliary arms, leaving AEF short of artillery. This had come about largely due to the clamour made by the Allies for the quick arrival of men. Consequently, arrangements with the French Command were necessary to secure the army and corps artillery, aviation and other services required for so important an operation.

The French involvement was: 2nd French Colonial Corps in the Richecourt to Mouilly sector, comprising the 39th Division, 26th Division and 2nd Dismounted Cavalry Division (all French). There was to be no division held in reserve, as the entire corps was to make follow-up attacks on the American advances.

In the St Mihiel salient German strength amounted to eight divisions and one separate brigade. Documents captured in June 1918, had shown that the enemy had a plan for evacuating the salient in case this became necessary. Prisoners and deserters, as well as abnormal activity noted by observers, now gave evidence that

At dawn 12 September 1918 the advance began; here infantry of the 1st Division moving up to the jumping off point. 86aUS (above) 85US (below)

The blown bridge at Flirey, blown up in 1914 by the French to stall the German advance. The Front Line and support trenches along with No Man's Land can be seen at top right. 88USa

the Germans had begun to move their artillery and ammunition dumps out of the salient in anticipation of an attack. Could they be caught with their field pieces out of position and on the roads?

The operation was initiated at 0100hrs, 12 September, by heavy artillery fire of unusual intensity. Through reinforcements of French artillery, the First Army had at its disposal 2,971 guns for the artillery preparation. Many of these guns were of heavy calibre, and the destruction and disorganization which it caused within the salient was enormous.

Forward!

At 0500hrs the six American divisions in the front line, on the southern face of the salient and west of the Moselle, advanced. This was preceded by a rolling barrage and assisted by French tanks, manned partly by American crews and partly by French. Tanks and Engineer detachments, equipped

A brigade headquarters beneath Flirey bridge. 88USa

with wire cutters and Bangalore torpedoes, went forward to cut the wire. To the American infantry the wire did not prove as great an obstacle as they had been led to expect. In many places the wire was old and badly kept up, some gaps had been cut by artillery fire, and paths made by the tanks. Above all, the Germans, demoralized by the volume of artillery fire and the suddenness of the attack, did not, except in certain sectors, put up a determined defence.

In a dash the Americans were over, under and through the German wire, which in just about every sector of the Western Front had held up the Allied advance for four years. It all seemed incredibly easy and all the initial objectives were taken according to plan. When it became evident that the attack was proving successful

Major General Joseph T. Dickman commander of IV Corps (1st, 42nd and 89th Divisions) during the battle of St. Mihiel. 89USa

In the St. Mihiel salient, Americans operating a French Chauchat machine gun (Model 1915). 90US

the whole schedule of attack was brought forward and the salient was neatly pinched out by a junction of the IV and V Corps in the vicinity of Vigneulles and Hattonville, effected early in the morning of 13 September.

In spite of heavy rains, which had made the ground soggy and difficult, many of the tanks managed to accompany the infantry over and through the German trench

This tank lunged through the German wire in advance of the 1st Division near Mont Sec, on the first day of the battle, before getting bogged down. The driver was Corporal George Heezh, Company C, 327th Tank Battalion. 93US

WW/US019b

89US

ESSEY

Tr. de la Reine

MORT MARE

1039

1239

Lauvaud Tr.

1234

WW/US019a

WW/US01

Top: American infantry advancing west of the village of Essey.
Above left: Aerial of the ground looking towards Essey over which the 89th Division attacked.
Middle right: Aerial of Essey while the Germans still held it.
Bottom right: French refugees in Essey after its capture.

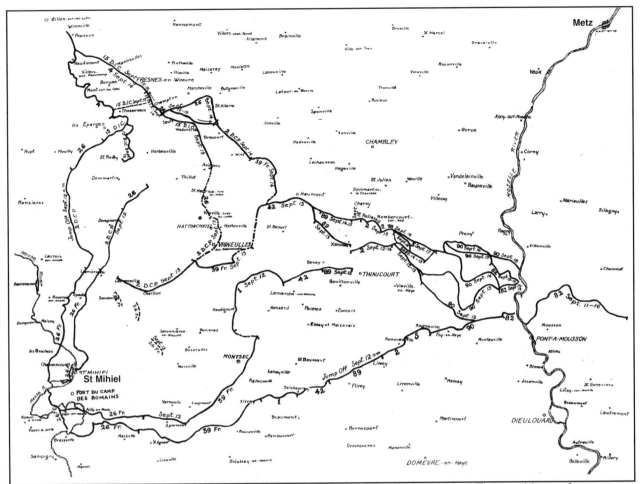

systems, neutralising machine-gun nests and pockets of resistance. The problem of supplying the advance over ground crossed by poor roads, which had been intersected by the trench systems and torn by shellfire, was great. Plus late, and particularly heavy rains had soaked the land, creating water-filled craters and clinging sludge. In these conditions commanders gave priority to lines of communication which in turn served to ensure momentum. The engineer companies had to face and overcome the difficult problem of assuring and maintaining the movement of artillery and all types of essential transport needed.

Command of the air was assured by upwards of 1,500 aircraft flooding the skies over and beyond the salient.

The advance was halted when the army objective was reached; and the defence of that objective was organized. A reconnaissance in strength was put into operation and that force pushed ahead in pursuit of the withdrawing Germans.

The outcome of the entire operation was the development in battle of the First Army as an effective weapon for future fighting. It had demonstrated to the Allied Command that, given the present state of the German defence capability, American troops could attack, and overcome, defenses on which four years of labour had

Searching the first batch of prisoners for papers and weapons before turning them over to the larger prison camp at Menil-la-Tour. Intelligence officers search through every scrap of paper, private letters, and postcards found on prisoners, for information that might reveal German intentions. These stockades were erected several days before the battle, in anticipation of the large haul of prisoners expected following a successful operation. 92US

Some of the first prisoners captured by the 103rd Infantry Regiment, 26th Division, on the first day of the attack on the German salient. WWI/US021

A sixteen year old prisoner affords some amusement. 94USa

No laughing matter. It seems the glum looking one in the middle protested against having picture taken 94USb

been spent. In a very practical way the gain was also important. The Paris-Avricourt railroad was free. More than 200 square miles of territory had been restored to the sovereignty of France. Captures in men and material amounted to 13,251 prisoners, 466 guns of all calibres, 752 machine guns, many trench mortars and small arms,

This picture was taken on the afternoon of the first day of the attack. A tank is being employed as a tractor to move a trailer.

ordnance material, engineering stores, quantities of ammunition, clothing and communications equipment and railway rolling stock.

The casualties for the First Army were about 11,000. Considering the numbers engaged and the results obtained, the losses were, in comparison to other military operations during the four years of fighting, remarkably light. Reserve divisions were committed to action in the direction of the Meuse-Argonne front as soon as the success of the St. Mihiel operation became obvious to all, and before it had ended completely. Front-line divisions were subsequently withdrawn for the same purpose, and the St. Mihiel front was permitted to stabilize.

Pressing the retreating Germans as they pull back in from the salient. 96US

Hattonchattel – it was near here that the 1st and 26th Divisions effected a juncture early in the second day of the battle. The salient was fast disappearing. WWI/US022

On street formerly named 'Hindenburgstrasse' these doughboys, flushed with victory, hold an *impromptu* naming ceremony. The place was Vigneulles where the juncture of the 1st and 26th Divisions spelled the successful pinching out of the salient.

Top left: A Signal Corps field battalion telephone switchboard. Captured German signals equipment can be seen on the table. 94USc

Left: Artillery spotter sending back information to the guns. Battery B, 21st Artillery, 5th Division. WW1/US023

Right: Lieutenant Colonel R. D. Garrett, 42nd Division, testing a German field telephone wire which they have failed to destroy in their rapid retreat. 98USc

Catching up on paperwork. This supplies officer has paused for 'ten minutes' in the advance; before he and his clerks carry on to find the front with his wagon train. 99US

Engineers returning from the front through shell-torn Nonsard. WWI/US024

When the American advance stopped, the French town of Thiaucourt, captured by troops of I Corps, came to be on the Front Line. The town had been fired by the Germans when they withdrew. They began bombarding it daily with gas shells; an example being, in one night they dropped five gas shells every minute for two hours. 102US and 101US

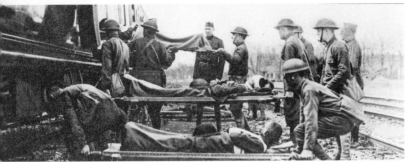

Carriages of an American hospital train used to transport wounded from the Front to base hospitals. 104aUS

Once aboard the train the wounded were in the midst of a well kitted out hospital on wheels. 104US

Slightly wounded men telling how it happened. Note the cross marked on the forehead of man sitting on the tailboard (right); this indicates that he is a gas victim. 100US

Brigadier General B. D. Foulois of the then called 'American Air Service', standing in front of one of the first Liberty planes to arrive in France. 103USa

A De Haviland D.H.4 observing over the St. Mihiel salient during the battle. WWI/US025

American flying field at Issoudon, France where many American pilots received their training. 103US

Flying officers who helped to make St. Mihiel a success story – pilots of the 9th Aero Squadron. 103US

Officers of 94th Aero Pursuit Squadron: Left is Eddie Rickenbacker, who would become the nation's leading ace with twenty-six confirmed victories (twenty-two aircraft and four balloons). Centre Lieutenant Douglas Campbell, and right, Captain Kenneth Marr. 80USb

Aerial photograph taken once peace had returned to St. Mihiel. The town was not badly damaged in the fighting as it was never bombarded directly by artillery from either side, although areas close to the river were bombed from the air. However, Chauvoncourt, opposite, across the river Meuse, was completely destroyed. Early in the war the French made an attempt to drive the Germans away from the town, but the attacking force had been severely disrupted when the Germans exploded a subterranean mine, killing many of the attackers. 105US

Men of the 35th Coast Artillery Company at Baleycourt, manning a 340mm calibre railway gun. They are attempting to hit the headquarters of two German Army Corps, near a railhead thirty kilometres north. Apparently, four shells were fired, and the air observer reported a direct hit for each of them. This railway gun was manned by 122 soldiers under the command of Major G. F. Humbert. 106US

Chapter Seven

Meuse-Argonne

FOLLOWING THE AMERICAN success in eliminating the St. Mihiel salient, the next step was to take over a portion of the front, and join in a general full-scale offensive about to be launched by the French and British. The strategic plan, agreed upon by the Allied commanders, involved an offensive which would cover the entire Western Front from the River Meuse to the English Channel. The main attacks for the Americans would be made astride the Meuse, thrusting through the Argonne in the direction Sedan-Mezières, and by the British and French in the north toward Cambrai-St. Quentin.

The American attack was to be supported on the left flank by the French Fourth Army between the Argonne and Reims. The attack would be launched on 26 September 1918. In the four years of

Two miles an hour was the rate at which traffic moved through Esnes near the Meuse-Argonne front. 108US

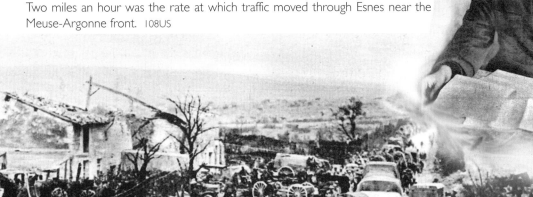

American manned French tanks moving up to the front near Boureuilles 26 September 1918.

fighting neither the French nor Germans had been able to force the other back, with the result that in September 1918, the German defenses were unusually deep and well-developed. German supplies and evacuations to and fro the Front in northern France were dependent upon two great railway systems; one in the north, passing through Liege, while the southern system, with tracks coming from Luxemburg, Thionville, and Metz, had as its vital section, the four-track line Carignan, Sedan,

Mezieres. Neither of these systems alone could supply the German masses in Northern France, and no other important lines were available to them because of the hilly terrain. The nature of the Ardennes had forbidden the construction of east to west lines through that region. In addition to the German dependence upon it for supply, that vital railway line was essential for the movement of troops. Were the Allies to sever the southern railway system the German armies would be in serious trouble.

From the Front Line, as it existed on 26 September 1918, the distance to the Carignan-Mezieres railroad line was about 50km. This region at that time formed the pivot of all German operations in northern France, and the vital necessity of protecting their four-track railway resulted in the convergence on the Meuse-Argonne front of several enemy defensive positions. Although, in the northern part of the sector the works were not so complete, the German defenses on the

Men of the 2nd Battalion, 307th Infantry Regiment, assembled one and a half miles behind their start point awaiting orders to move up. IIIUS

Secretary Baker, and Major General J.W. McAndrew, observe the questioning of a captured German officer by intelligence officers 1st Lieutenant Jennings, and 2nd Lieutenant McCoy. Information gleaned at such cross-examinations would greatly assist in the coming Allied offensive. Information sought included the enemy order of battle, his strength, condition, morale, strength of his positions and condition of his reserves. 112US

Meuse-Argonne front consisted of trenches to a depth of 20km or more. East of the Meuse the dominating heights not only secured the Germans' left flank, but afforded him ideal positions in which powerful artillery could be sited to bring an enfilade fire on the western bank. German artillery batteries, located in the elaborately fortified Argonne forest, secured their left flank, and could even cross their fire with those of the German guns on the east bank of the Meuse.

Midway between the Meuse and the Argonne the heights of Montfaucon afforded the Germans excellent observation, and formed a strong natural defensive position, which had been substantially fortified. Behind Montfaucon, wooded heights constituted natural features which were also most favourable to the defence, and unfavourable to those seeking to overturn it. Not the least of the difficulties faced by the First Army attackers was the breadth of No Man's Land, along with the total

AEF FIRST ARMY ORDER OF BATTLE

III CORPS
33rd, 80th, 4th, Divisions
3rd Division in reserve

Army reserve: 1st Division

V CORPS
79th, 37th, 91st, Divisions
32nd Division in reserve

Army reserve: 29th Division

I CORPS
35th, 28th, 77th, Divisions
92nd Division in reserve

Army reserve: 82nd Division

Army reserve
5th French Cavalry Division

2,775 guns supported the attack
189 tanks (142 manned by Americans)
821 aircraft (604 manned by Americans)

destruction of roads across that entire area. A daunting prospect for an American military success. Nevertheless, an attack at this point of the German line would compel the them to reinforce in strength, resulting in the advance of the Allies farther west benefiting. Perhaps, it was reasoned, if the combat-fresh American troops could win a victory in this sector, victory would finally be in sight.

Planning
The original intention for the Meuse-Argonne operation would involve fifteen divisions. Of these the 1st, 3rd, 4th, 35th, 80th, 82nd and 91st had taken part in the

Tanks of the 326th Battery, 311th Tank Center, moving up to take their place ready for the attack. 114US

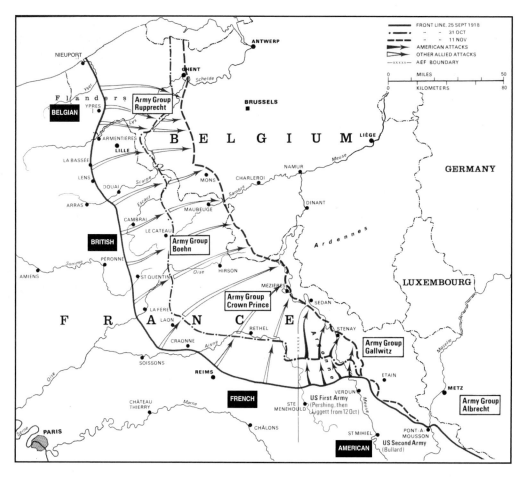

St. Mihiel offensive; the 29th, 37th and 92nd were in the Vosges sector; the 28th, 32nd and 77th were in the neighbourhood of Soissons; the 79th Division was in the American training area and the 33rd was near Bar-le-Duc. A daunting task for the American First Army planning staff, to gather all the divisions for the forthcoming Allied attack. To ensure secrecy, all movements had to be made at night, and as only three routes were available the roads were jammed to capacity.

On 22 September, command of the Front from east of the Meuse to the western edge of the Argonne, passed to the American First Army, with its headquarters at Souilly. Also command of the French XVII Corps, comprising three divisions, passed to American First Army. The army front now extended from east of the Moselle river to the western edge of the Argonne. The Meuse-Argonne front had been taken over from the Second French Army which had rendered valuable assistance in routing troops stocking ammunition and establishing supply dumps. Eventually the First Army stood ready on the night of 25 September 1918.

The Germans facing them had ten of their divisions in the line and ten in reserve

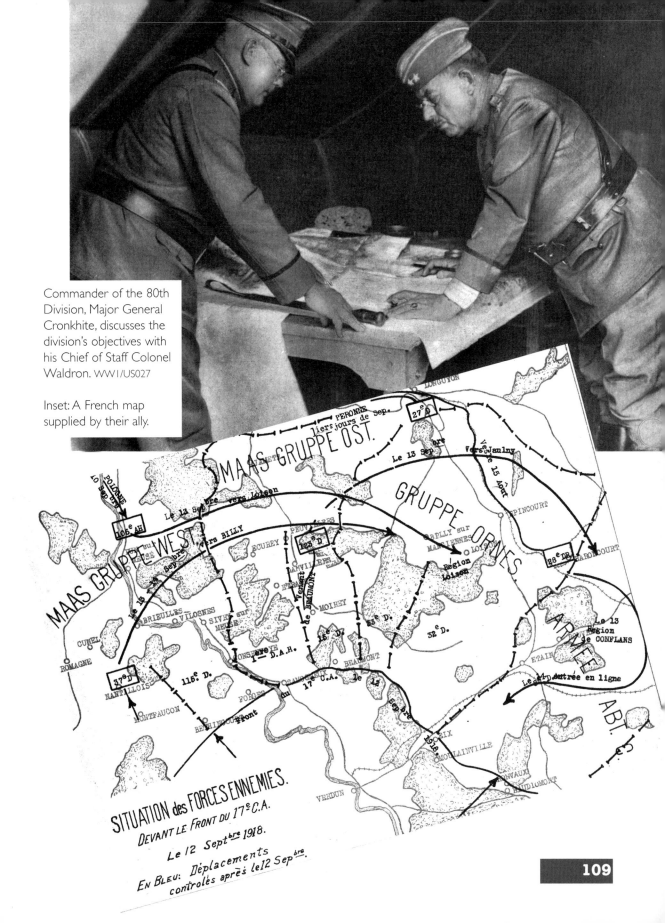

Commander of the 80th Division, Major General Cronkhite, discusses the division's objectives with his Chief of Staff Colonel Waldron. WWI/US027

Inset: A French map supplied by their ally.

on the front Fresnes-en-Woevre-Argonne Forest. Following the American success at St. Mihiel the Germans expected a further offensive initiative against them – but where would it fall? A series of successful ruses east of the line of the Meuse, extending as far south as Luneville, had deceived the Germans and as a consequence the actual attack came as a tactical surprise. The surprise feature had been assisted by an arrangement whereby French troops manned the American First Line until the last possible moment before launching the attack.

The Meuse-Argonne Offensive
Artillery interdiction fire on communications in the rear was begun six hours before the initial infantry attack. Three hours before the attack fire was increased and intense artillery preparation all along the front commenced. At 0530hrs on 26 September the artillery preparation changed to a rolling barrage, and the infantry advanced.

In securing total surprise it had meant that a long artillery preparation with tanks

The quick-firing French 75mm field gun, because of its recuperator system, could be fired at speed without the need to relay it after every shot. It is reputed that one captured German officer requested to see the weapon that could fire shells like a machine gun. 132US

SPAD 11 a French two-seat biplane reconnaissance aircraft flown here over the lines by the crew of an American squadron. 118US

leading the infantry, at least in the initial stages, were not possible. Therefore, the infantry was dependent upon its own resources for cutting through the elaborate German system of barbed wire. This slowed the infantry advance, as did the difficulties of the terrain. Nevertheless, the infantry progressed without encountering serious resistance, except before Montfaucon. The early overrunning of the enemy's first positions, led to the hope that the 5th French Cavalry Division, in army reserve, might be pushed through the line to exploit the success in the

A 340mm gun manned by the US Coast Artillery Corps firing into the German lines from the area of Nixeville, 26 September 1918. WWI/US030

direction of Grand Pre. However, blocked roads and other causes prevented the cavalry from getting through before the enemy reorganized his defence. The cavalry did not reach Varennes, and the 5th Cavalry Division (French) took no further part in the fighting.

French lancers ready to follow up a German retreat. A remarkable photograph of a mounted group moving towards the camera. The original caption admits that cavalry no longer played an important part in war. However, in the event of a great retreat, the horsemen would a play great part in pursuing the enemy and prevent the consolidation of new lines. WWI/US031

Engineers of the 28th Division repairing a bridge at Boureuilles blown up by the Germans.
WWI/US032

The success of the initial assault having been assured, the critical problem became the movement of artillery and ammunition across the trackless No Man's Land to support the continued progression of the troops. Also the strong point of Montfaucon, which had not fallen on the 26th, interfered with moving guns forward. However, at 1100hrs on 27 September, the 79th Division captured Montfaucon and the centre of the line went forward. At the same time the American extreme left was meeting strong resistance in the

Their first objective taken, members of Company B, 108th Machine Gun Battalion, 28th Division are halted for a rest near Boureuilles, 26 September 1918.
Left: not dead just exhausted.
WWI/US033a and 33

Argonne. The attack continued without interruption and the Germans, recognizing the danger, threw six new divisions into line on 29 September. Supported by massed machine-gun fire and backed by heavy artillery fire, numerous counter-attacks with fresh troops were launched by the Germans. The brunt of which was born by the 28th and 35th Divisions.

By nightfall of the 29 September, the First Army line was approximately Bois de la Cote Lemont-Nantillois-Apremont, south-west across the Argonne. Some of the American divisions had suffered severely. Units had become intermingled due to the difficult nature of the ground over which they had attacked and which the fog, smoke, and the fall of night had aggravated. Relief of these attacking divisions had to be made before another coordinated general attack could be launched. Consequently, on the night of 29 September, the 37th and 79th

Major General Charles H. Muir, 28th Division.
WWI/US034

Men of the 308th Infantry Regiment, 77th Division resting in a captured German trench after their first day advancing in the Argonne region. 110US

Divisions were relieved by the 32nd and 3rd Divisions respectively, and on the following night, the 1st Division relieved the 35th Division.

At 0530hrs 4 October, the general assault was renewed, and within days the battle was extended to the east of the Meuse, which was in pursuance of instructions received to increase the extent of the battle front and draw in more German divisions.

On 8 October the French made a general attack on the front, east of the Meuse, with the

Varennes, taken on the first day of the Meuse-Argonne battle by the 28th and 35th Divisions, comprising men from the Pennsylvania and Missouri National Guard. 115US

From the ruins of Varennes, Battery C, 108th Field Artillery, 28th Division, fires on retreating Germans. 113US

following divisions in line from right to left: 26th French Division, 18th French Division, and American 29th and 33rd Divisions. That attack fell on a vital point – the pivot of the huge German salient formed by their entire incursion into northern France. The Allied attacking troops encountered elaborate fortifications and near desperate resistance.

On 9 October, American V Corps attacked with the 1st Division, reinforced by one infantry brigade of the 91st Division and the 32nd Division; the stubbornest defence was encountered, and fighting was intense, but an advance was made. On the 10th the Argonne was cleared.

Huge mining craters in No Man's Land at Vauquois Hill, where in previous fighting French and German miners had fought an underground war, attempting to break the four year deadlock.
Inset: Colonel Harry S. Howland, Commanding Officer of the 138th Infantry, who was awarded the DSC, the Croix de Guerre, and the Cross of the Legion of Honour for gallantry in action on this hill.   WWI/US035a and 35

The outskirts of the village of Cheppy. The advance is going well and this transport company is able to take a break. 116US

On 18 October there was heavy fighting east of the Mouse, and the offensive continued everywhere by local operations. On the 23 October, the III Corps and V Corps pushed northward as far as Bantheville. It was now necessary to relieve certain troops, consolidate positions, and generally to get forces and supplies in hand before attempting another general attack. The remaining days of October were spent by the Americans preparing for the great attack scheduled for 1 November 1918.

Results so far

The material results that had been obtained by the American First Army up to the end of October, could be summarized as follows: The Germans' most elaborately prepared positions had been broken through; the southern half of the Argonne was back in French hands; 18,600 prisoners, 370 cannon, 1,000 machine guns and countless material of all sorts captured; an increasing number of German divisions had been drawn into the fight; the great German military railway, the artery through

In 1918, from 20 to 30 per cent of all American battle casualties were due to inhaling poisonous gas. This staged photograph was arranged to serve as a graphic warning of the consequences of not wearing a gas mask. 117US

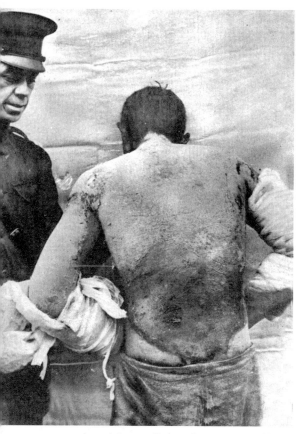

A soldier suffering from mustard gas blistering. WWI/US036

Carigan and Sedan, was seriously threatened. Also, there were the morale results: the American soldier had proved himself in battle. The American Expeditionary Force had developed into a powerful and smooth running machine, and everyone, from the Commander-in-Chief to the latest arrival in France from the States was confident of the ability of the American soldier to carry through any task. On the other hand, the morale of the German soldier had been seriously reduced until his will to resist had reached the breaking point. He was ripe for the disaster which was about to overtake him.

Elsewhere

By early October the ration strength of the American First Army, including the French troops, had risen to over a million men, and the organization of another army became necessary. On 10 October the Second Army was created, and on 12 October Major General Robert L. Bullard was assigned to command it. The St. Mihiel front, extending from Port-sur-Seille to Fresnes-en-Woevre, was taken from the First Army and assigned to the Second Army. On 12 October the Commander-in-Chief assigned Major General Hunter Uggett to command the First Army.

In light of the gains there was the prospect of forcing an early conclusion to the war. Consequently, it was decided to keep all troops in line to the utmost of their powers of endurance, and thereby forbade the rest to which the tired divisions were entitled. Seriously weakened divisions which could no longer remain in the battle-front were therefore sent to the calmer sector of the Second Army. Despite the fact that it was constantly composed of tired divisions, the Second Army managed to keep the Germans directly in its front on the alert. The Second Army was preparing to launch its own powerful offensive when all plans were stopped on 11 November by the armistice.

When the British attacked on 8 August 1918, on the Amiens front, America was represented there by the 33rd Division.

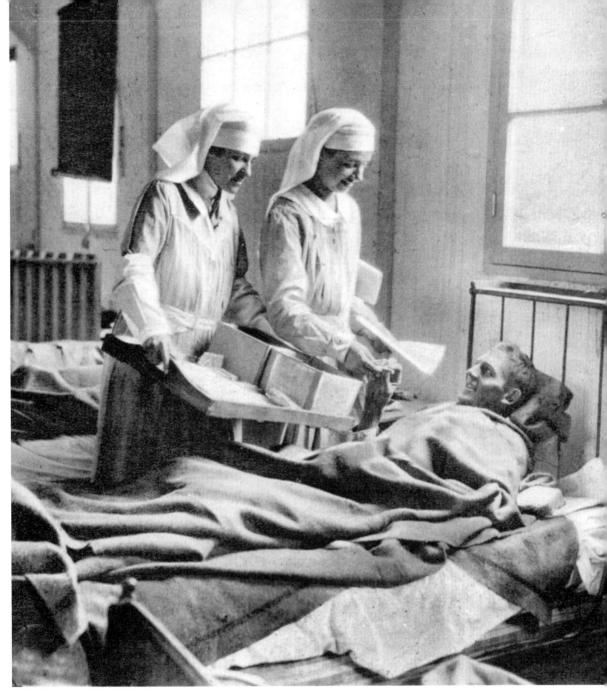

An American is ministered to by two nurses from Aberdeen, Scotland, Miss Anderson and Miss Marie H. Jowett. This was taken at the evacuation hospital, Fleury-sur-Aire. 119USa

'Big Nims' of the 3rd Battalion, 366th Infantry, finds great amusement in the grotesque appearance of a buddy with a gas mask adjusted over his face and head. WWI/US037

Forgetting the fighting, this sergeant is gaining much pleasure in scrounging for souvenirs; the German *Picklehaub* being the favourite item in his collection. 119US

When the First Army was formed at St. Mihiel, the III Corps with the 28th, 32nd and 77th Divisions had been left on the Vesle. Early in September (3rd to 13th) the 28th and 77th Divisions attacked, and as usual progressed. On 29 August the 32nd Division, which had entered the line north-west of Soissons attacked, and by its success it aided the advance of the French on both of its flanks. The 6th, 81st and 88th Divisions held sectors in the Vosges during September and October, the last division being relieved on 4 November, II Corps with the 27th and 30th Divisions remained on the British front until the armistice. These two divisions played an important part in breaking the Hindenburg line, and when the armistice was signed they had taken nearly 6,000 prisoners, 44 guns and over 400 machine guns.

A first aid dressing station near Nantillois. 121USa

Ruins of the village of Cuisy captured by the 4th Division. Lightly wounded Americans are in the rear of the truck and some seriously wounded Germans are on the stretchers. 123US

German and American dead collected for burial.
121USb and 121US

The Fourth French Army, attacking west of the Argonne, requested American troops. To comply with this request the 2nd Division entered the French line on 30 September and on 3 October attacked a strong position and on the first day broke through to a depth of 6km. This allowed the French on either flank to advance. The 2nd Division not only held the positions it had gained, but made further progress until its relief on 10 October by the 36th Division. The 2nd Division had taken 2,296 prisoners and the 36th Division, which had never been in the line before, showed what it was capable of when it had reached the Aisne after an advance of 21km. In October, at the time the Americans were heavily engaged in the Argonne, Pershing received an urgent call from Marshal Foch for two American Divisions to help the French Sixth Army and the Belgians, who were attacking in the extreme north. In answer to that call the 37th and 91st Divisions were promptly sent north, and were there when the armistice took effect on 11 November.

Final offensive

The French Fourth Army and the American First Army had felt the need of a period of comparative inactivity, so that the troops might be reorganized and supplies accumulated for another joint and concerted attack. The first day of November had been selected for that attack. The general objective was still the region Sedan-Mezières, and its primary purpose was to cut the all-important German military artery – the railway line. The first and immediate objective of the First Army was

Artillery observers in an advanced position are spotting for the 16th Field Artillery, 4th Division, near Nantillois. 122US

Corporal Erland Johnson, 58th Infantry at the north-west edge of Bois de la Cote Lemont during 4th Division's advance in the Argonne. 124US

Left: General William Lendrum Mitchell, Chief of the Air Services, AEF. In the Second World War the North American B-25 bomber was named the 'Mitchell', after him – a unique honour. 135US

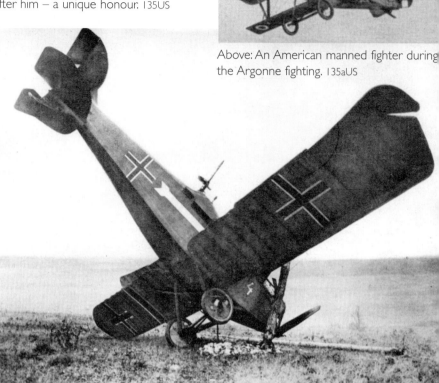

Above: An American manned fighter during the Argonne fighting. 135aUS

Captain Eddie Rickenbacker wearing his recently awarded DSC. By the end of the Argonne campaign he was the American top ace with twenty-six aerial victories. 120USa

Above: Hannover CL.III a two-seater multi-role aircraft, primarily used as a ground attack machine. This was shot down by American machine gunners. 125US

Left: Lieutenant Frank Luke, credited with bringing down four aircraft and fourteen observation balloons. He was killed after crashing and refusing to surrender. 128US

Inset: Leutnant Ernst Schultz, one of Luke's victims brought down near Verdun. 128USa

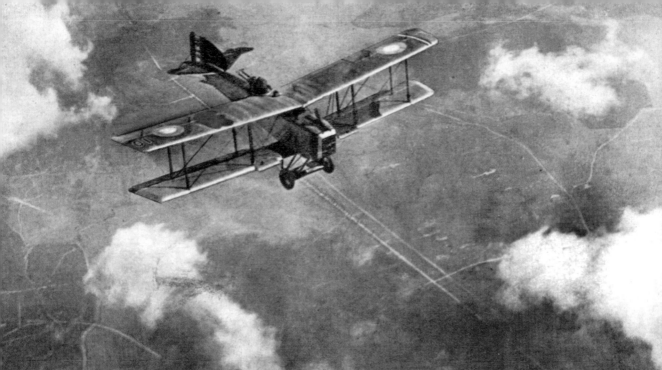

The French Breguet XIV was a highly successful biplane used by the American Air Services. Designed by Louis Breguet in 1916; it was one of the first aircraft constructed with Duralumin in the airframe. 126US

the capture of Buzancy and the heights of Barricourt, the outflanking of the northern part of the Argonne, and establishing contact with the French Fourth Army near Boult-aux-Bois.

The attack was preceded by two hours of concentrated artillery bombardment in support of the infantry. The result was that the Germans were overwhelmed and broke; III Corp took Andevanne, and V Corps pushed forward and drove the defenders from the heights of the Bois de Barricourt, a formidable natural obstacle which had blocked the way to Sedan. On 3 November, III Corps troops were rushed forward in motor trucks in pursuit of a

Bombing Montmedy, 42km north of Verdun 127US

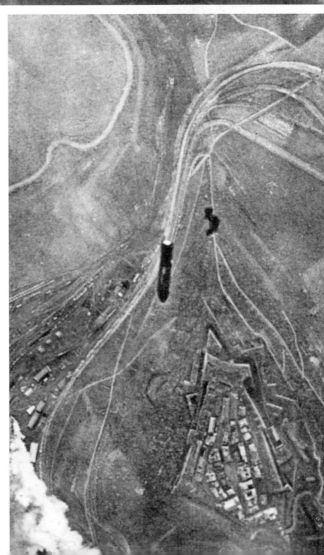

Guns crews of 313th Field Artillery, 80th Division, about to move the 75s into position in woods near Nixeville. 129US

Opposite: During the Meuse-Argonne Offensive, Sergeant Cullum Alvin York was one of the most decorated American soldiers in the First World War. He received the Medal of Honor for leading an attack on a German machine-gun nest, capturing thirty-two machine guns, killing twenty-eight Germans and capturing 132 others. As an elder in a Tennessee mountain church, York had considered himself a conscientious objector, and could not bring himself to take the life of a fellow human, but he experienced a drastic change of heart. It was said of him that he was the 'greatest individual fighter of the war'.

WWI/US038

Bringing in the prisoners. Twenty-three thousand German prisoners were taken during the operations of the First Army in the Meuse-Argonne sector. 131USa and 131US

demoralized enemy. St. Pierremont was taken, and V Corp had taken Fosse and III Corps Beauclair. The German line had been broken to a distance of 20km. Heavy batteries were rushed forward to fire on the important railway lines at Montmedy–Longuyon Conflans. The ultimate object of the whole operation was within reach. On 4 November the pursuit was continued, and operations were extended to the east bank of the Meuse. German resistance was completely disorganized; all his reserves had been committed and his first-line divisions were in retreat. To the east of the Meuse, however, the enemy still held, and progress was slow. On 6 November, I Corps pushed 7km beyond Raucourt, the great railway artery was within artillery range. A continuation of such operations, and those

In eleven days of almost continuous fighting American casualties in the 1st Division amounted to 8,500. The territory captured was 7km along the Aire valley and included Fleville and Exermont. This is a street in the village of Exermont where a dead German lies in the road. The Germans were about to begin shelling the village when this photograph was taken. 326US

of the Allies further north, meant the end of all the German Armies in Northern France.

Since 7 October, a date which coincided with that on which it became certain that German forces could not wrest from the American First Army its initial success in breaking the Meuse-Argonne line; the German Government had sought by way of the President of the United States to secure an armistice, which, needless to say,

German machine gunner on the Hindenburg Line who carried out his orders and fought to the last. 134USa

Two machine gunners in the 90th Division operating a British Vickers machine gun in support of the 358th Infantry, attacking the German line in the Bois des Rappes, 20 October 1918. 137US

View of Granpre and the Valley of the Aire, as seen by the German defenders manning machine guns along the hillside. The amount of expended cartridge cases indicates the ferocity of the fighting here. The entire strong point bristled with machine guns which poured a continuous stream of fire on the attacking Americans as they came up the trough of the Aire. The Americans took the position on their fourth attempt. 140US

would in the German mind be acceptable to Germany. Several exchanges of notes between the German Government and President Wilson took place until finally, on 5 November, the President informed Germany that the question of an armistice must be taken up with Marshal Foch, the Allied Commander-in-Chief. On 6 November, when the First Army had driven German forces back so hard until the retreat became a rout, the German High Command asked Marshal Foch for a conference. The German representatives met Marshal Foch on the night of 7 November. The Germans asked for an immediate cessation of hostilities. Marshal Foch refused, and gave the Germans seventy-two hours in which to accept armistice terms which had already been prepared. The Allies were ordered to continue to attack. The move of the Germans toward an armistice served to hasten all Allied preparations for the delivery of a final blow in case the enemy did not accept the terms offered him and on the 11 November the six divisions needed to

The type of German defensive positions along the Krimhilde and Hindenburg Lines that the Americans had to overcome in their advance. Bodies of the defenders litter the ground after the positions had been captured. 138US and 138USa

support the left of the French were enroute to the right bank of the Moselle to join in the attack, which was scheduled for 14 November.

On 7 November, the river line of the Meuse, to a point not far from Sedan was in the hands of the American V and I Corps. On the same day the German forces on the heights south-east of Stenay were pushed back into the plain of the Woevre. The attack of the American First Army was now directed toward Carignan, I Corps

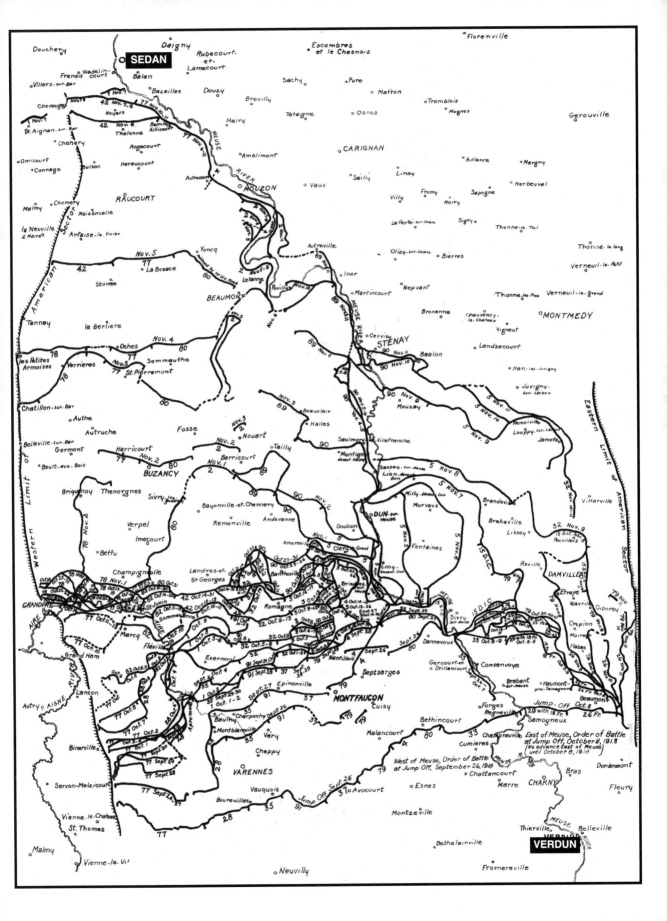

Château de Sedan. At least six American divisions and one French division had been racing to be the first into Sedan, with elements of the 1st and 42nd American capturing the hills overlooking the city on 7 November, and were planning to take it the following day. Orders from Marshal Foch ordering them to withdraw stopped the Americans taking it. 146US

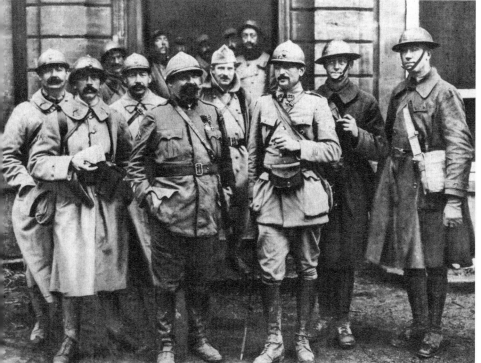

On 7 November, American officers (83 Infantry Brigade) had requested of the French that they might be allowed to accompany them into Sedan, when it became known that the Germans had left. The French agreed, but higher French command decreed otherwise. French hearts were involved with the border town. During the Franco-Prussian War, 2 September 1870, the French emperor Napoleon III was taken prisoner with 100,000 of his soldiers at the First Battle of Sedan. Reoccupying the place after forty years was to be an event for the French alone.

WWI/US040

Graves at Cheveuges of the last Americans to be killed in front of the town of Sedan. 142US

was withdrawn, and its sector taken over by the Fourth French Army. East of the Meuse the pursuit was continued. On 10 November, V Corps forced a crossing over the Meuse, south of Mouzon, and on the morning of the 11th they crossed at Stenay and occupied that town in liaison with III Corps on its right.

Early on the morning of 11 November, the German commissioners accepted the terms of the Armistice; American General Headquarters was at once notified by Marshal Foch's headquarters that the armistice would go into effect at 1100hrs. The Armies were at once informed, and they in turn transmitted the order through the Corps headquarters to the troops. The advance had been so rapid that communication beyond Corps headquarters was uncertain, and in at least one case one small detachment took prisoners after 1100hrs.

From 26 September to the end of hostilities on 11 November the Germans committed forty-six divisions in their attempt to defend the Meuse-Argonne sector. This amounted to a quarter of their entire divisional strength on the Western Front. American casualties were around 119,000.

11 November 1918, 1059hrs: 'Calamity Jane' 11th Field Artillery, positioned at the Bois de la Haie fired off her last shell of the war. 148US

Right: At 1101hrs this gun section of battery D, 105th Field Artillery, after firing its last shot, hoisted the Stars and Stripes to loud cheering. 149US

'It was the attack of the American troops west of the Meuse that, with the impetuosity which the German Staff had not believed possible for them upon so short a period of training, had gained the decision for the Allies and brought about the ruin of the German Army.'

German General Staff Officer.

Chapter Eight

Victory and Armistice

IN THE MONTH of September 1918, Germany began to break under the Allied offensives delivered by the overall commander Marshal Foch. Evidence of weakening became apparent after Prince Maximilian of Baden became Imperial Chancellor of Germany on the 3 October. Two days later he addressed a note to President Wilson asking him to notify the Allies that Germany desired an Armistice.

The American High Command at General Headquarters. Front row, left to right: Brigadier General H. B. Fiske, G 5 (Training Section); Major General J. W. McAndrew, Chief of Staff; General John J. Pershing, Commander in Chief; Brigadier General Fox Conner, C 3 (Operations Section); Brigadier General G. V. H. Moseley, G 4 (Co-ordination of Supply Service). Rear row, left to right: Brigadier General A. D. Andrews, C 1 (Administrative Section); Brigadier General Leroy Eltinge, Deputy Chief of Staff; Brigadier General D. E. Nolan, G 2 (Information Section); Brigadier General R. C. Davis, Adjutant General. 150US

As the world war was coming to an end something akin to the Plague swept the earth. The 1918 influenza (the 'Spanish flu') was an unusually severe and deadly pandemic that spread across the world. Most victims were healthy young adults, in contrast to all previously known influenza outbreaks, which mainly affect juvenile, elderly, or weakened patients. It lasted from June 1918 to December 1920, spreading even to the Arctic and remote Pacific islands. Between 50 and 100 million died, making it one of the deadliest natural disasters in human history. Even using the lower estimate of 50 million people, 3 per cent of the world's population (1.86 billion at the time) died of the disease. A nurse attends patients at Camp hospital No.45, Aix les Bains, Savoie, France. WWI/US042

In accordance with this request the matter of terms was submitted to the Supreme War Council sitting at Versailles.

The first formal meeting between the Allied powers took place at Versailles on 13 October. Representing the United States were General Tasker H. Bliss and Admirals Benson and Sims. The terms agreed upon were completed on 4

The war ended here at 0500hrs Monday, 11 November 1918. The German representatives headed by Secretary of State, Mathias Erzberger, signed the Armistice terms in Marshal Foch's private railway carriage, No. 2419 D. The train, to which the car was attached, stood on the track at the station of Rethonde, in the Forest of Campiegne. Marshal Foch was accompanied by his Chief of Staff, General Weygand and Admiral Sir Rosslyn Wemyss, First Sea Lord of the British Admiralty.   WWI/US044

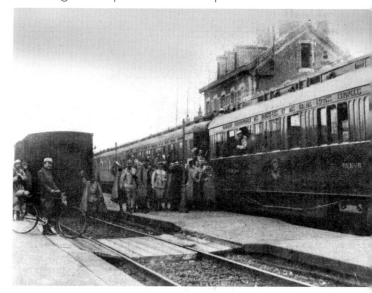

November and on the following day President Wilson notified the German government that Marshal Foch had been empowered to receive German envoys, and communicate to them the conditions on which an Armistice would be granted. Three days of communication by wireless followed between Paris, and the German Great Headquarters at Spa, Belgium, in which arrangements were made for German delegates to cross the lines. The latter presented themselves on the 11 November at Marshal Foch's field headquarters, a railway carriage in the Forest of Compiegne, which was standing on a side track at Rethondes railway station. Germany was represented by Secretary of State, Mathias Erzberger, General H. K. A. Winterfeldt, Count Alfred von Overndorff, General von Gruenell and Naval Captain von Salow. Along with Marshal Foch were Admiral Sir Rosslyn Wemyss, First Sea Lord of the British Admiralty, and General Weygand, Chief of Staff to Foch.

When, at 0500hrs the Armistice terms were accepted, and forms were signed, word was immediately sent by telegraph cable, telephone and wireless to all parts of the world.

General Pershing, in his final report to the Secretary of War, described receipt of the news at American General Headquarters:

> *At 6 o'clock am on the 11th notification was received from Marshal Foch's headquarters that the Armistice had been signed and that hostilities would cease at 11 am. Preparatory measures had already been taken to insure the prompt transmission to the troops of the announcement of an Armistice. However, the advance east of Beaumont on the morning of the 11th had been so rapid, and communication across the river was so difficult that there was some fighting on isolated portions of that front after 11 am.*

The last sentence explains why some American elements were still engaged after 1100hrs, a feature that aroused some criticism at the time. By the terms of the Armistice the Allies were to occupy German territory on the west bank of the Rhine, with bridgeheads on the east bank of 30km radius at Cologne, Coblentz and Mainz. American forces were assigned the territory around Coblentz, with that city

American Army of Occupation, 149th Field Artillery, 42nd Division, crossing the Sauer River from Luxembourg and entering into Germany. WWI/US045

as headquarters. Under orders from Marshal Foch, General Pershing put his troops on the alert, readying them for a march to the Rhine on 17 November. Especially for the tasks ahead, the American commander-in-chief hastily formed a Third American Army, known as the Army of Occupation, and placed at its head, Major General Joseph T. Dickman, who had been a division and corps commander during the months of fighting.

Following through the Grand Duchy of Luxembourg, close upon the heels of the retreating Germans, the American Third Army crossed the Sauer and Moselle Rivers into Rhenish Prussia, on 24 November. Signal Corps and ambulance units were the first elements to cross the border. The advance guard of the main army entered Trier on 1 December. Unruly elements in the Coblentz region gave cause for concern with the possibility of an uprising. To forestall this, and at the request of German authorities, on the 8 December, a battalion of American troops was rushed by special train to Coblentz. Thereafter, American forces moved into the occupied territory according to schedule and settled down for their 'Watch on the Rhine'. At first the population was sullen, but gradually friendlier relations came about.

The next step in legally ending the First World War was the Peace Conference

The mighty *Festung Ehrenbreitstein* Rhine fortress, situated across the river from the headquarters of the American Army of Occupation. The fortress occupies the rocky heights above the busy German waterway. Because of the fear of revolution the German civil authorities requested the Americans to take over security as soon as they reached Coblentz. The observation balloon belongs to 3rd Balloon Company, 1st Division, and is observing up and down the Rhine.   WWI/US046

President Wilson and President Poincare leaving Paris railway station, 14 December 1918. WWI/US047

to be convened in Paris. President Wilson, accompanied by a large staff of diplomats and advisers, sailed for France on the USS *George Washington,* landing at the port of Brest on 13 December 1918. The representatives of the United States – other than the President, at the Peace Conference, were, Robert Lansing Secretary of

Palace of Versailles, where crowds can be seen gathered about the palace gates on the occasion of the signing of the Peace treaty, 28 June 1919.   WWI/US043

State; Henry White, former ambassador to France; Edward N. House and General Tasker H. Bliss.

Paris gave President Wilson a tremendous ovation when he arrived on the 14 December and drove through troop-lined streets to the home of Prince Murat, where he resided during his first stay in France. Before the opening of the Peace Conference, the president visited England and Italy, being received everywhere with great warmth by the populace. Various sessions were held at the Quai D 'Orsay, home of the French Foreign Ministry up until 13 January 1919. Thereafter, the sessions continued, until the terms finally agreed upon were signed by the German plenipotentiaries, in the Halls of Mirrors at the Palace of Versailles on 28 June 1919.

In the interval between the cessation of hostilities and the signing of the treaty of peace with Germany, the American Army command was occupied with caring for the well-being of 2,000,000 soldiers, impatient to return to their homes.

It had taken nineteen months to transport 2,079,880 American troops to Europe, but the exodus from France was much more rapid. The backward flow did not get fully under way until April, 1919. By September of that year the last division, the 1st, was back in the United States. This photograph shows the 87th Division, one of the earliest outfits to begin the return trip home, embarking on the transport *Manchuria* at St. Nazaire, 10 January 1919. 152US